Elizabeth Warren's
BIG, BOLD PLANS

LAURIE ANN THOMPSON

illustrated by SUSANNA CHAPMAN

Atheneum Books for Young Readers
NEW YORK LONDON TORONTO SYDNEY NEW DELHI

As a child, Elizabeth Warren never dreamed she would one day run for president of the United States. She had a different big, bold plan:

She would be a teacher.

Eisenhower

Truman

Roosevelt

Hoover

Coolidge

Elizabeth enjoyed school and did well. So well, in fact, that her second-grade teacher took note. She asked Elizabeth to work with some of the other students on their reading. When Elizabeth helped a classmate learn a new word, she felt a great sense of accomplishment. She was hooked!

From then on, she taught anyone who would listen.

Elizabeth was the baby of the family, and the only girl. Her daddy had a steady job, and her mother took care of the home. She had a happy childhood. But her world took a frightening turn when she was twelve years old.

It was a cold, gray Sunday evening. Elizabeth's daddy came in from working outside. She was struck by his stillness, his shaking hands, his splotchy skin.

"We're going to the hospital," her mother told her. "You stay here." With only her little dog, Missy, to comfort her, Elizabeth waited and worried. Later, she heard two dreadful words: heart attack.

Her daddy came home, but he wasn't able to work for a long time. Bills piled up. They couldn't pay for their car anymore, so the bank took it away. Would their house be next? Just in time, her mother got a job. Elizabeth helped too— waiting tables at her aunt's restaurant and sewing dresses. The family made it through those tough times, together.

Not long afterward, Elizabeth started high school. She had skipped sixth grade, so she was younger than the other kids. And those kids lived in big houses and wore fancy clothes, while her family was barely scraping by. How could she possibly fit in?

Elizabeth refused to let her worries get the best of her. She joined as many clubs and activities as possible, and soon found herself exactly where she belonged:

ON THE DEBATE TEAM.

Preparing for a debate required hours of research and practice.

The competitions taught her to think logically, speak clearly, and stay calm under pressure. Elizabeth loved rising to each challenge.

Those skills would come in handy if she became a teacher as planned, but she would need to go to college. Her mother didn't approve of the idea. She wanted Elizabeth to get married and raise a family. And Elizabeth couldn't afford college anyway.

Still, she had to try: She researched universities that gave money to students who excelled at debate. She applied, got accepted, and then persuaded her mother to let her go. At sixteen, she moved across the country to attend George Washington University.

HER PLAN WAS STILL ON TRACK.

Two years later, Elizabeth's high school boyfriend asked her to marry him.
She was a teenager in love, and she didn't want to disappoint her mother.

Elizabeth said yes. She dropped out of college, and the couple moved to
Houston, Texas. But Elizabeth wasn't happy—she still wanted to teach.

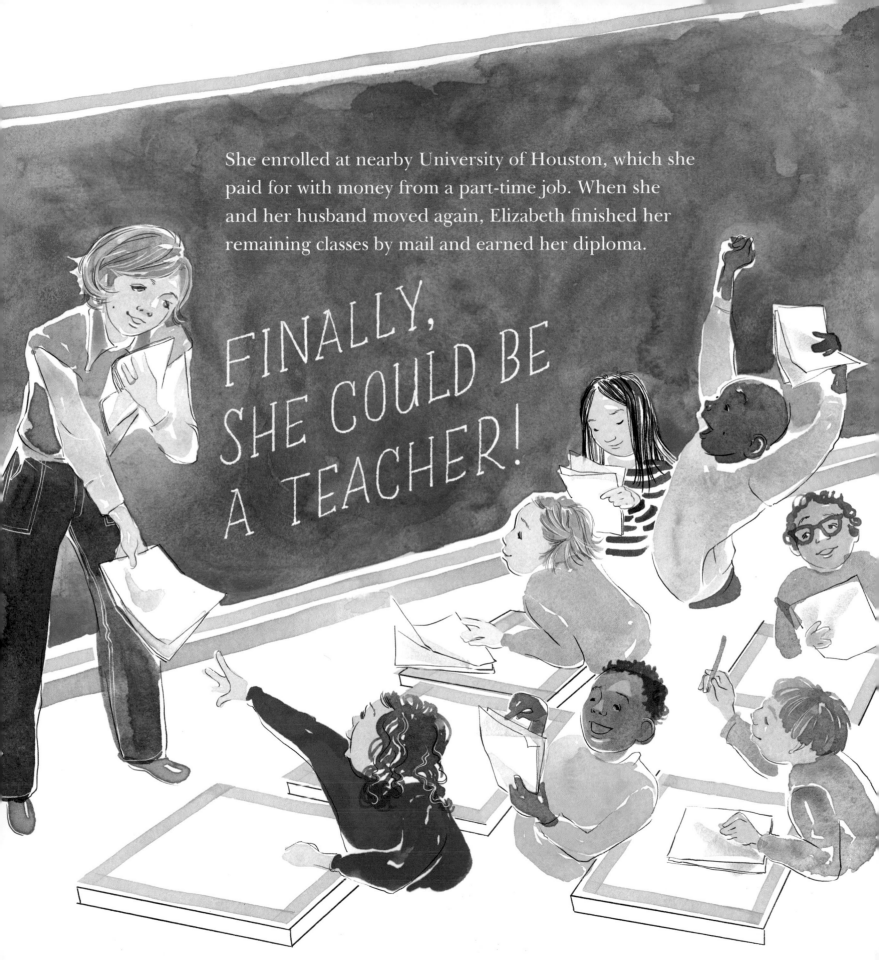

She enrolled at nearby University of Houston, which she paid for with money from a part-time job. When she and her husband moved again, Elizabeth finished her remaining classes by mail and earned her diploma.

FINALLY, SHE COULD BE A TEACHER!

Elizabeth loved helping her students, but it didn't last long. After the school learned she was going to have a baby, they gave her job to someone else. After all her hard work, her dream of teaching seemed to have hit a dead end.

WHAT COULD SHE DO?

Elizabeth still wanted to use her skills to help others,
so she found another career that could give her
the same sense of accomplishment:

SHE WOULD BE A LAWYER.

Her classes were challenging, but Elizabeth threw herself into the work and graduated from Rutgers Law School shortly before her second child was born. Law firms weren't interested in hiring a woman with young children, so she took matters into her own hands and hung a sign in front of her house. She had become a lawyer to help people, and she would do that from her own living room if she had to!

Then her law school called. They needed to hire a teacher, and one of her professors had recommended her! After all the twists and turns and bumps in the road, Elizabeth's big, bold plans merged together in an unexpected way: She would be a teacher after all, and she would be a lawyer, too. She would teach her students how to

USE THE LAW TO

HELP PEOPLE. It was perfect.

Several years later, a new law passed that affected people who couldn't pay their bills. Elizabeth was curious. She remembered her own family's struggles when she was young. If they had gotten through it, she wondered, why couldn't everyone else? To understand, she would have to do her research.

What she found surprised her: story after story of people who had worked hard but simply had some bad luck . . . a heart attack, a lost job, or a divorce. From there, things went from bad to worse. Desperate to pay their bills, people borrowed money from banks. The more money they borrowed, the harder it was for them to pay it back. Elizabeth realized the rules had changed: Working hard wasn't always enough anymore. New laws protected banks more than they protected people.

IT WASN'T FAIR.

That newfound knowledge gave Elizabeth a new mission.
People were hurting—people not that different from her
own family—and it didn't seem like anyone in power cared.
But Elizabeth cared. She told their stories every chance she got.

She wrote articles and books. She gave interviews and speeches. She wanted people in power to do something to help those with none. She wanted the country's leaders to care about its citizens as much as she did.

NOTRE DAME LAW REVIEW
1980

WASHINGTON UNIVERSITY LAW REVIEW
2004

AS WE FORGIVE OUR DEBTORS
BANKRUPTCY AND CONSUMER CREDIT IN AMERICA

All Your Worth
Elizabeth Warren &
Amelia Warren Tyagi

And it worked . . . for a while. Politicians passed laws to protect working people and made rules to keep the banks in check. But in 2005, everything changed again. New laws made it easier for banks to trick people and make unsafe business deals. New rules made it harder than ever for people who were just trying to get by.

By 2008, so many people couldn't pay back the money they had borrowed that the banks found themselves in big trouble. That put the whole country— in fact, the whole world— in trouble too. There was no choice: The government had to save the banks. They asked Elizabeth to oversee how that was handled. She was nervous. She wasn't a politician! But she was a teacher and a lawyer, and this was her chance to teach the country's leaders that

LAWS SHOULD HELP PEOPLE.

When she finished that job, President Barack Obama himself asked Elizabeth for help. He wanted her to create a brand-new agency, one that worked to protect people's money. Elizabeth hesitated. It was an incredibly complex task, and everyone would be watching. But she knew the issues inside and out, and she cared about the millions of people affected by them. There was only one choice: She had to try. And she succeeded.

After that remarkable achievement, many people wanted her to run for the United States Senate. Again, Elizabeth wasn't sure. Politics had never been part of her plans . . . but helping people was. She knew that, as a senator, she would be able to make an even bigger difference for the people who needed it most. She was still nervous, but

SHE DECIDED TO RUN.

It was a big dream, but Elizabeth
fought hard—and she won!
As the first woman senator for
Massachusetts, she kept listening
to people's stories. She kept
working to fix rules that
were unfair. She kept helping
people in need. She was
a mother, a teacher, a
lawyer, and a United
States senator. She had
done more than
she'd ever dreamed.

But it was no longer just about her.

Elizabeth knew there were more changes she wanted to make, more problems she wanted to solve, more people she wanted to help. She started dreaming about her biggest, boldest plan yet:

TO RUN FOR PRESIDENT.

It would take a lot of hard work, but she was used to that. She started making even bigger, bolder plans: plans to make it easier for workers to earn and keep more money; to give every American an equal chance to achieve their dreams; and to help all of them be safer, healthier, and happier. She wanted to put power back where it belonged:

IN THE HANDS OF
THE COUNTRY'S CITIZENS.

Elizabeth Warren has been making plans her entire life. As a child, she never dreamed she would one day become a United States senator or run for president. Still, her persistence and empathy led her there—

ONE BIG,

BOLD

PLAN

AT A TIME.

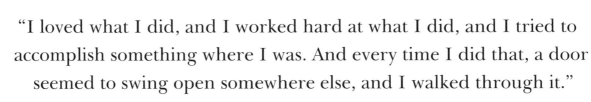

"I loved what I did, and I worked hard at what I did, and I tried to accomplish something where I was. And every time I did that, a door seemed to swing open somewhere else, and I walked through it."

— *Elizabeth Warren*

Timeline

1949: born to Donald and Pauline Herring, joining brothers aged four, twelve, and fifteen

1962, spring: father has heart attack when Elizabeth is twelve

1962, autumn: enters high school at age thirteen in Oklahoma City, Oklahoma

1966: graduates high school at age sixteen with a debate scholarship to George Washington University in Washington, DC

1968: marries Jim Warren at age nineteen; drops out of college; moves to Houston, Texas

1970: graduates from University of Houston with speech pathology and audiology degrees

1971: daughter, Amelia, is born

1976: graduates from Rutgers Law School in Newark, New Jersey

1976: son, Alex, is born

1977–78: is a lecturer at Rutgers Law School

1978: divorces from Jim Warren

1978–83: teaches at University of Houston Law Center

1980: marries Bruce Mann

1983–87: teaches at University of Texas at Austin, Texas

1987–95: teaches at University of Pennsylvania Law School in Philadelphia, Pennsylvania

1989: publishes *As We Forgive Our Debtors*

1992: is a visiting professor at Harvard Law School in Boston, Massachusetts

1995: starts teaching at Harvard Law School

1995: is asked to advise the National Bankruptcy Review Commission

1996: registers as a Democrat

2003: publishes *The Two-Income Trap* with her daughter

2006–10: is a member of the FDIC Advisory Committee on Economic Inclusion

2008: is appointed to lead a Congressional Oversight Panel to review the implementation of the Emergency Economic Stabilization Act

2010: is named assistant to President Barack Obama and special adviser to the Secretary of the Treasury on the Consumer Financial Protection Bureau

2012: runs for United States senator from Massachusetts and wins; is first woman to hold that office

2014: publishes *A Fighting Chance*

2016: declines to run for president of the United States and endorses Hillary Clinton instead

2017: is rebuked by Senator Mitch McConnell ("Nevertheless, she persisted.")

2017: publishes *This Fight Is Our Fight*

2019: announces 2020 campaign for president of the United States

Select Bibliography

Felix, Antonia. *Elizabeth Warren: Her Fight, Her Work, Her Life*. Sourcebooks, Inc., 2018.

Rutgers University Newark. "Interview with RU-N Alumna Elizabeth Warren." YouTube. November 9, 2011. Accessed October 18, 2019. youtu.be/NItCGcV84GM.

Traister, Rebecca. "Elizabeth Warren's Classroom Strategy." The Cut. August 6, 2019. Accessed August 26, 2019. thecut.com/2019/08/elizabeth-warren-teacher-presidential-candidate.html.

Warren, Elizabeth. *A Fighting Chance*. New York: Henry Holt and Company, 2014.

———. *This Fight Is Our Fight: The Battle to Save America's Middle Class*. New York: Henry Holt and Company, 2017.

Author's Note

I have admired Elizabeth Warren for years, so I enjoyed getting to know her a bit better while doing research for this book. I was surprised to learn how many things we have in common. We were both born in June. We were both youngest daughters raised in middle-class families in small, rural communities. We were both rough-and-tumble girls who did well in school. We both ended up pursuing completely different careers than what our public university degrees would suggest. We both love dogs! And we both try to help others and solve problems.

Warren seems to me to exemplify what a politician—no matter what party or ideology they represent—should be: someone who is truly in it to serve, to help people, to make the world a better place. I am very grateful for those genuine public servants who work so selflessly across so many levels of our government.

Of course, no politician is perfect. They are, after all, human, and they make mistakes just like the rest of us. Do I agree with everything Warren has ever said or done? No. I don't even agree with everything *I* have ever said or done! We are all, hopefully, learning and growing and trying to do better every day. Warren has acknowledged her mistakes, apologized when necessary, and changed her mind when presented with new evidence. That is why I am excited to see her out there trying to help people, trying to do the right thing, trying to lead our country forward. I'm excited to see her run for president of the United States. And I'm excited to see what she'll do after the election, because, win or lose, I'm sure she will have big, bold plans.

ATHENEUM BOOKS FOR YOUNG READERS ★ An imprint of Simon & Schuster Children's Publishing Division ★ 1230 Avenue of the Americas, New York, New York 10020 ★ Text copyright © 2020 by Laurie Ann Thompson ★ Illustrations copyright © 2020 by Susanna Chapman ★ All rights reserved, including the right of reproduction in whole or in part in any form. ★ ATHENEUM BOOKS FOR YOUNG READERS is a registered trademark of Simon & Schuster, Inc. Atheneum logo is a trademark of Simon & Schuster, Inc. ★ For information about special discounts for bulk purchases, please contact Simon & Schuster Special Sales at 1-866-506-1949 or business@simonandschuster.com. ★ The Simon & Schuster Speakers Bureau can bring authors to your live event. For more information or to book an event, contact the Simon & Schuster Speakers Bureau at 1-866-248-3049 or visit our website at www.simonspeakers.com. ★ The text for this book was set in Baskerville BT. ★ The illustrations for this book were rendered in watercolor and Photoshop. ★ Manufactured in the United States of America ★ 0320 WOR ★

First Edition ★ 10 9 8 7 6 5 4 3 2 1 ★ Library of Congress Cataloging-in-Publication Data ★ Names: Thompson, Laurie Ann, author. | Chapman, Susanna, illustrator. ★ Title: Elizabeth Warren's big, bold plans / Laurie Ann Thompson, Illustrated by Susanna Chapman. ★ Description: First edition. | New York : Atheneum Books for Young Readers, [2020] | Includes bibliographical references. | Audience: Ages 4–8 | Audience: Grades 2–3 | Summary: "A picture book biography of Senator Elizabeth Warren"— Provided by publisher. ★ Identifiers: LCCN 2019055473 | ISBN 9781534475809 (hardcover) | ISBN 9781534475816 (eBook) ★ Subjects: LCSH: Warren, Elizabeth—Juvenile literature. | Women legislators—United States—Biography—Juvenile literature. | Legislators—United States—Biography—Juvenile literature. | United States. Congress. Senate—Biography—Juvenile literature. | United States—Politics and government—21st century—Juvenile literature. ★ Classification: LCC E901.1.W37 T46 2020 | DDC 328.73/092 [B]—dc23 ★ LC record available at https://lccn.loc.gov/2019055473